31 Days
of Prayer
for
My Teen

Books by the Yates family:

And Then I Had Kids: Encouragement for Mothers of Young Children, Susan Alexander Yates

And Then I Had Teenagers: Encouragement for Parents of Teens and Preteens, Susan Alexander Yates

Character Matters! Raising Kids with Values That Last, John and Susan Yates

How a Man Prays for His Family, John W. Yates

The Incredible Four-Year Adventure: Finding Real Faith, Fun, and Friendship at College, John Yates III and Chris Yates

Building a Home Full of Grace, John and Susan Yates and Family

31 Days of Prayer for My Child, Susan Alexander Yates and Allison Yates Gaskins (available 2005)

31 Days of Prayer for My Teen

A Parent's Guide

SUSAN ALEXANDER YATES

BakerBooks
Grand Rapids, Michigan

© 2004 by Susan Alexander Yates

Published by Baker Books
a division of Baker Publishing Group
P.O. Box 6287, Grand Rapids, MI 49516-6287
www.bakerbooks.com

Printed in the United States of America

Library of Congress Cataloging-in-Publication Data

Yates, Susan Alexander.
    31 days of prayer for my teen : a parent's guide / Susan Alexander Yates.
       p.   cm.
   ISBN 0-8010-1271-6 (pbk.)
    1. Teenagers—Prayer-books and devotions—English. I. Title: Thirty-one days of prayer for my teen. II. Title.
   BV4850.Y38 2004
   242′.845—dc22   2004009761

To our Father God, who loves to hear our prayers
no matter what!

And with special thanksgiving to him
for the five spouses he has given our five children:

Will Gaskins, Christy Borgman, Alysia Ponzi,
Scott Anderson, and McLean Wilson

I've prayed for each of you since you were infants.
I didn't know you then, but God did,
and he has answered my prayers above and beyond
anything I ever dreamed in bringing you
into our lives.

To him be the glory!
Ephesians 3:20–21

Contents

Acknowledgments

A big thank-you to my husband and best friend forever, John. A special thank-you to our five children: Allison, John, Chris, Susy, and Libby, who taught me to love the teen years. And heartfelt thanks to my editor, Vicki Crumpton, and the great team at Baker Books.

About the Book

As parents of teens we know we need to pray, but we are often so overwhelmed with all our child's needs (and our own!) that we don't know where or how to begin.

This book will help you!

You'll find two ways to use this book. First, you can use it as a daily prayer for your teen by matching each day to the day's date. With this method you'll be able to cultivate the habit of regular daily prayer for your teen, and in the process you'll experience the joy of a regular time to let God himself love and encourage you. By praying in this way, you will receive the benefit of exploring prayers and issues that might not have occurred to you.

Second, you'll note that each prayer has a particular topic so you can go directly to the topic that expresses your concern and pray that specific prayer. Prayers are listed by topics in the table of contents.

The inspiration for this book came from a book I wrote several years ago called *And Then I Had Teenagers: Encouragement for Parents of Teens and Preteens*. That book deals with the challenges we face as we raise our teens. In it you will find practical guidance in handling many of the issues that you will be praying about in this book. I hope you will use this book of prayers as a companion to the larger book. Additional help is also available in the book my husband and I wrote, *Character Matters! Raising Kids with Values That Last*. Further information about these two books and other helpful resources can be found in Appendix 4 in the back of this book.

In the prayers I have tried to balance my use of *he* or *she* and *son* or *daughter*. I felt that using *he/she* repeatedly would be distracting, so I have chosen one or the other to use in each prayer. Please adjust the gender to suit your needs.

At the end of each prayer you will find activities that can personalize and deepen your prayer time. First there is a relevant Scripture verse. Second, a list of additional Bible verses, which are referenced in the prayer, will expand your study. Let the printed prayer be a basis for creating your own prayer for your child each day, and then write it in the space provided. You will be encouraged when you use the book next month to see how God has answered your prayer! Next, thank God for one of his character traits that has been brought to your mind by the prayer or by the verses. (For example, *Thank you, God, that you are always faithful.*) Throughout the day, take time to think about what his *faithfulness* means to you. Space is also provided to write out a promise from God encountered in your Scripture study. Use these tools to enhance your time with God.

Perhaps praying for your child is a new experience for you, and you may be thinking, *I'm not even sure I ought to be talking to God. I don't feel that I know him in the same way others do.* If this is a question in your heart, I invite you to turn to Appendix 1 in the back of the book for some personal encouragement before you begin to pray for your teen.

One of our greatest desires is that our teens come to know Christ personally. In Appendix 2 you will find a prayer that you can use to pray for your child's faith.

Appendix 3 contains a driving contract that may be helpful to you when your teen begins to drive.

In Appendix 4 you will find a list of other encouraging resources for this season of parenting teens. Each resource is accompanied by a brief description.

However you choose to use this book, I pray that you will find yourself not simply going to God with the latest issue about your teen but also falling in love with a God who cares about every detail in your teen's life—*and* in yours.

Introduction

My children have been the most instrumental growth factor in my walk with Christ. When five kids arrived within seven years, I was overwhelmed and exhausted. When they reached the teen years, I was scared silly. And I was driven to my knees in a more intense and frightened way.

I was forced to ask honest, hard questions. *Could I really trust Christ with my children? Would he hear my prayers, even if they were wrong, even if I felt unworthy to pray, even if the problem was me? Did he care? Would he help?*

I truly believe that God hasn't given us the kids we have merely so that we might raise them. He's given us the exact kids he has in the exact birth order with the exact personalities so that they might also be used as his tools in our lives to mold us into the men and women he has created us to be. He's given us that strong-willed son, that daughter with disabilities, that child who is so much like us that we are constantly at each other's throats, that child who is so different that we can't understand him, and yes, even that stillborn child. Not one is a mistake. Each child is a precious gift from God. And each child will be used by him to grow us up into the men and women he longs for us to become.

We may or may not feel adequate in our profession. We can succeed, quit, or get fired. Marriage, with its challenges and blessings, is still between two equal adults who, with Christ at the center, can build a strong union. *But raising kids is oh so different.*

We have the burden of responsibility from the beginning. We can shape fragile souls or damage tender hearts. Even the most successful person in the world's eyes will come to his knees in the arena of parenting. Parenting is the most humbling calling in the world, for here we cannot deny our own failings.

In those times of agony and tears on my knees crying out on behalf of a child, I have sensed God's presence as I have at no other time. Yes, I have come face-to-face with my own brokenness. No, I haven't always seen quick solutions or easy answers. Guidance hasn't often come instantly. More often I've had to wait and wait on him. Often silence has been my companion. Sometimes I haven't even felt that God hears.

In those times I've learned to go by faith. *It's not about my feelings; it's about his character.* He hears. He loves. He understands. And he is at work in my teen's life and in mine. In times of fearing, in times of weeping, and in times of rejoicing, I have opened the window to my soul and let him minister to me in the most tender place of all—the heart of a parent.

As you use this little book to help you in praying for your teen, I pray that the eyes of your heart would be freshly opened and that you too would come to believe in a deeper way that *the Lord is trustworthy.*

> *He tends his flock like a shepherd:*
> *He gathers the lambs in his arms*
> *and carries them close to his heart;*
> he gently leads those that have young.

ISAIAH 40:11, EMPHASIS ADDED

Moody Teen

Teenagers are moody. There's no getting around it. Hormones are raging; emotions are near the surface. Some teens withdraw; others overwhelm you. And the same child can switch personalities daily. How is a parent to respond? Be comforted in knowing you are not alone.

Lord, I'm exhausted by living with these mood swings. I never know "who" is going to walk in the door after school. Will my daughter be "up" because the "right girls" asked her to sit with them at lunch, or will she be in a bad mood that screams "get out of my way" because a certain boy did not speak to her in the hall?

I feel held captive by these mood swings. I feel guilty from the feeling that somehow I'm supposed to make her happy and I can't. Her moodiness is making us all walk on eggshells. It's impacting everyone in the family. It's like she's on a constant emotional roller coaster. I don't know if this is a normal teenage disposition or if it has crossed the line to unacceptable. Should I ignore it and ride it out or deal with it? And if I ought to deal with it, I need you to show me the best way. Living with a moody person who's always changing is so hard. I can't seem to count on anything.

Father, my daughter's moodiness reminds me that I too can be moody. I go up and down in my relationship with my family and, yes, even with you! I need your help for me as well as for my daughter.

O Lord, thank you that you aren't a moody God. Instead you are the same yesterday, today, and forever.* I can count on you. You are solid. You don't change.* You are full of compassion* and yes, righteous anger, but also unfailing love.* You have promised to give me wisdom when I don't know how to handle a teenager.*

Father, I ask that you would show me how to handle my moody teen. Please give me your supernatural wisdom today.

> *Jesus Christ is the same yesterday and today and forever.*
>
> HEBREWS 13:8

Scripture references (in order of starred references in prayer): Hebrews 13:8; James 1:17; Lamentations 3:22; Psalm 107:1; James 1:5

My prayer for my teen today:

16

The character trait of God that I will focus on today:
(Thank you, God, that you are . . .)

One promise of Scripture for today:

Unlovable Teen

A parent can be shocked to realize that at this moment, she doesn't like her teen very much. It makes us feel ashamed and guilty. But in most homes it's a reality. We'll be most helped by being honest about our feelings and taking them to our heavenly Father, for he truly understands.

Lord, I don't like my teenager. I know I'm supposed to love him, but how can I love him when I don't even like him? He seems unlovable. He resists me on every front. He is not fun to be with. He doesn't want to be with me, either. He lets me down over and over again. And when I try to show him love, he turns away. It hurts so much.

Lord, you must know exactly how I feel. Too often I act just like my child. I ignore you. I don't spend time with you. I let you down. I think I can handle things by myself. And when you reach out your arms to me, I turn away. I hurt you, O Lord. I too am unlovable.

But even then you, O Lord, are still full of love for me. You demonstrated your love when you gave your Son Jesus for me.* You illustrated the power of your love when you enabled Hosea to love the unlovable prostitute Gomer and take her as his wife even though she continued to turn away from him.* You are the God who calls us from our unlovable waywardness and who offers love freely.* You alone, O God, can fill me with love for this unlovable child.*

As I dwell on your love for me, in a sense "your unlovable teenager," please give me your loving heart for my own child. Show me today specific things in him that I can love. Remind me of positive traits that he does have! Help my attitude toward him not to depend on his response. Instead, help me to rely on the unlimited love flowing from you to me to my child that cannot be stopped.

May your unfailing love be my comfort,
according to your promise to your servant.

PSALM 119:76

Scripture references (in order of starred references in prayer):
John 3:16; the book of Hosea; Hosea 14:4; Psalm 107:8–9

My prayer for my teen today:

The character trait of God that I will focus on today:
(Thank you, God, that you are . . .)

One promise of Scripture for today:

False Teachers

I n today's culture so much is being taught as good, proper, or advanced that is in fact deceitful, false, and corrupt. Yet too often false teaching comes disguised in noble terms and seemingly loving actions. Sexual immorality, dishonesty, and even nudity are presented as funny and normal by the media. We parents have no way to stay on top of all that's out there. We can no longer interpret or monitor everything for our kids. We need help.

Lord, protect my teen from the subtle influences of false teachers. In this postmodern age we're so easily taken in by persuasive people who teach untruth. It can be hard to recognize what is false when it's so attractive and so "in," so politically correct and so acceptable. Often the lies seem so intellectual while truth is portrayed as too simplistic or too arrogant. The deception is so subtle. Sometimes I worry that my child could be taken in by a false worldview instead of understanding culture from a biblical perspective. I fear that she might not even recognize what is happening.

I too can be taken in by false values and deceitful lies without even realizing it. Make me alert, dear God. Show me today where I'm being deceived or where I'm compromising. Keep me sharp and alert to the truth. Help me to see false teaching for what it really is, and give me the courage to stick to your truth.

I am so glad, O Lord, that you aren't wishy-washy. There is a truth, and you are it!* You aren't shocked or thrown by false teachers.* You know that we and our children will face them and their persuasive teachings.* Yet your truth is stronger than the world's lies.

Lord, you want my child to walk in the truth even more than I do. Please help my child to recognize false teaching.* Whisper truth into her ear. Put into her path people who will speak your truth, especially people to whom she will be drawn and to whom she will listen.* Protect her from buying into that which is false. Instead, help her to resist and to overcome. Grow her up into a woman whose confidence in you cannot be shaken.

His anointing teaches you about all things and as that anointing is real, not counterfeit—just as it has taught you, remain in him.

1 JOHN 2:27

Scripture references (in order of starred references in prayer): John 14:6; 2 John 7–8; 1 John 4:4–6; 1 John 4:1–3; Proverbs 4:11

My prayer for my teen today:

The character trait of God that I will focus on today:
(Thank you, God, that you are . . .)

One promise of Scripture for today:

Starting to Date

Social customs are ever changing. Some kids go out in groups, some go out in pairs, some don't go out at all, and it happens at different ages! But at some point our kids will want a date for the prom, the homecoming dance, a special event. Where will it lead? Will it lead to wholesome relationships or dangerous entanglements?

O Father, as my teen starts to go out on dates, I'm fearful! I don't know if she's ready for this. I know I'm not! What if she doesn't make wise decisions, falls for the wrong type of guy, goes "too far" physically? What if she gets used or gets her heart broken? O Lord, the stakes are so high. This could impact her whole life!

I so easily focus on the "what ifs." They are a tool of the enemy to lead me to fear. How easily I fall prey to them. You have promised to give me faith for today, one day at a time.* This is stretching me to trust you in new ways, O Lord, but you have promised to help me when I have a hard time trusting.*

I know you understand my fears, Lord.* I can't protect her, but you can.* Deliver her from life-damaging decisions. Give her healthy interaction with boys. Teach her how to relate to them. Give her wholesome friendships and a deep appreciation for men. Guard her heart.* Save it for the one you are preparing for her. (I do ask, God, that if it would please you, you would bring her a husband!)

And Lord, I pray for her future husband. Please keep him in your care. Help him to be growing to love you with all his heart. Surround him with Christian friends and mentors. Keep him pure until marriage. Prepare him for the specific job you have for him. Guide him to make wise choices. Give his parents wisdom as they raise him. Bring him into her life in your perfect time. Wherever he is today and whatever he is doing, I ask that you would protect him. Give him a desire to resist temptations and instead to seek you with all of his heart.*

"My Spirit, who is on you, and my words that I have put in your mouth will not depart from your mouth, or from the mouths of your children, or from the mouths of their descendants from this time on and forever," says the LORD.

ISAIAH 59:21

Scripture references (in order of starred references in prayer): Matthew 6:11, 34; Mark 9:24; Psalm 147:5; Psalm 37:24; Proverbs 4:23; Matthew 7:7–11

My prayer for my teen today:

The character trait of God that I will focus on today:
(Thank you, God, that you are . . .)

One promise of Scripture for today:

In a "Potential" Relationship

Most likely our teen will fall in love someday. We don't know when that "someday" will be, and we can't do much about it. But if it comes early, we may have some anxious thoughts. Is my child ready? Is this the right person for my teen to spend the rest of his life with?

Dear Father, my son really seems serious about this girl. I can tell that his affection is growing. His heart is being wooed. He genuinely cares about her. She could even be "the one." She knows you, and she seems crazy about my son. Yet even though they are both believers, this still may not be the match you desire.

Lord, I don't know if this is right, but you do! And they don't know yet either, even though they might think they do! You know each of them intimately.* You know their strengths and their weaknesses. You know if they will fit together. You know the plans you have for them.*

Lord, if it is not your desire that this relationship lead to marriage, I ask you to break them up. Give one of them a deep lack of peace. Show one of them that this is not of you. Give one of them the courage to break up. How this will hurt, O Lord. I ask you to gently hold the broken hearts and surround them with comfort—not with comfort as the world gives but with your supernatural comfort.*

Lord, this could well be the right person but the wrong time. If this is so, I ask that you would give one of them the strength to take a break, to call things off for several months and use that time to seek your will. And during the time apart, I pray, let each come to know you and your love in deeper ways than ever before. In your time, please clearly show them your will for their relationship.*

But, Lord, this could be it! If it is your perfect will for these two to marry, I pray that you would continue to confirm it in every area. Keep them both seeking you individually and together. Give patience where it is needed. Guide them in the timing and details of marriage. Most of all, overwhelm them with awe that you are doing something wonderful!*

Now to him who is able to do immeasurably more than all we ask or imagine, according to his power that is at work within us, to him be glory in the church and in Christ Jesus throughout all generations, for ever and ever! Amen.

EPHESIANS 3:20–21

Scripture references (in order of starred references in prayer):
Psalm 139:1–5; Psalm 40:5; 2 Corinthians 1:3–5; John 7:17;
Ephesians 3:20–21

My prayer for my teen today:

The character trait of God that I will focus on today:
(Thank you, God, that you are . . .)

One promise of Scripture for today:

In a Dangerous Relationship

A relationship our teen has with the opposite sex may cause us great agony. We may instinctively know that this relationship is not right. In fact, we fear for our child. We see what she is doing, and we see a tragedy in the making. We need God's intervention.

Father, my heart is heavy. The relationship my daughter has with this boy is not good. He does not know you. She's not seeking you right now either. She knows what is right, but she has set your truth aside. She's too "in love" to listen to anyone. She thinks she knows her own heart, but she has no idea what she's doing.*

O Lord, I feel so helpless. I've said all I can to her. I can't say any more, and she wouldn't listen anyway. She's withdrawing from me. She says it's her life and that I don't understand or know everything.

Lord, you know her heart.* Underneath all her confusion she does know you. She's heard your truth, and your truth has power.* Please light in her heart the flame of your truth that she has let smolder. Give her a heart that isn't divided between following you and having this boy.*

Father, I pray that if she doesn't have the strength to break this relationship off, he would. Throughout history you have worked through nonbelievers to let believers go. I remember the pagan king Artaxerxes letting Nehemiah go.* Breaking up a relationship is easy for you. Lord, I also ask that you would send into her life a wise, godly person whom she will listen to. (It's surely not me!) Give someone the courage and the opportunity to talk to her about this relationship. Father, if this is not the right match, I ask you to do whatever it takes to end this relationship.

I will give them an undivided heart and put a new spirit in them; I will remove from them their heart of stone and give them a heart of flesh. Then they will follow my decrees and be careful to keep my laws. They will be my people, and I will be their God.

EZEKIEL 11:19–20

Scripture references (in order of starred references in prayer):
Jeremiah 17:9–10; Psalm 139:23; Ephesians 1:19; Psalm 86:11; Nehemiah 2

My prayer for my teen today:

The character trait of God that I will focus on today:
(Thank you, God, that you are . . .)

One promise of Scripture for today:

On a New and Risky Adventure

Our teens have to become independent, pursue new directions, and yes, even take risks. It's hard on us, because it involves letting go, and we don't like that. We're used to being there, to overseeing, to guiding. But we can't always do that. It would be unhealthy.

Lord, today I'm just plain scared. My child is off on this new adventure. It's filled with opportunities for growth but also with potential risks and dangers. I'm not there, and I can't protect him. I feel so helpless, so frightened. It's hard to trust you with my teen, to believe that you will protect him as he takes this risk. Protecting him has been my job all these years (at least it felt like it was my job—I know it was really yours). But this is different. It's so much harder. I'm not there.

What if he doesn't show good judgment? What if he gets hurt? What if he dies? Not every story has a happy ending.

What if mine doesn't? Lord, I am really frightened of the unknown. I realize I don't know what will happen. Instead I have to learn to trust that you are who you say you are.

You are my refuge and fortress.* You love my son even more than I do. You are watching over him day and night. You don't even sleep; instead you are watching over him this very moment.* You delight in his well-being!*

Protect him today, dear Father. Help him to look to you.* Put your angels around him to guard him.* Help him to see your hand in what he's doing and to sense your presence. And help me to grow in trusting this dear son into your care, for you will always be with him, and I can't.

So do not fear, for I am with you; do not be dismayed, for I am your God. I will strengthen you and help you; I will uphold you with my righteous right hand.

ISAIAH 41:10

Scripture references (in order of starred references in prayer): Psalm 91:2; Psalm 121:1–8; Psalm 35:27b; Psalm 91:14; Psalm 91:11

My prayer for my teen today:

The character trait of God that I will focus on today: (Thank you, God, that you are . . .)

One promise of Scripture for today:

Friends

Friends are one of our teen's great needs and at the same time one of our big concerns. What if our child doesn't have any? What if we don't like the ones she has? What if they are a bad influence? How do we handle their peer pressure?

O Father, you know how important friends are to my teen. And you know how influential they can be! I used to have the most influence with my daughter, but now she listens to her peers instead of me. She tells them things she used to tell me. I feel shut out. Depending on who she's hanging out with, I'm either grateful or terrified. I know this is normal, Lord, but it's still hard.

Father, you understand the importance of friends. You had twelve disciple-friends. And of those twelve you had three best friends, Peter, James, and John. Even you, the Son of God, needed friends. And I think of Moses with his partners, Aaron and Hur, and how Paul had Silas and Barnabas and how David had Jonathan.

Father, I ask that you would give my child good friends, not friends who will pull her away from you but instead friends who love you and want to grow in you. Protect her from bad company who might corrupt her.* Give her a hunger to seek out healthy friendships and an aversion to unhealthy ones. At the same time, Father, give her compassion for people unlike herself. Protect her from being "cliquish." Help her to learn to be a good friend to others.*

In particular I pray for her friends _____, _____, and _____. I pray that you would draw them to yourself.* Give them courage to stand strong.* Help them to sharpen each other.* Lead them in the paths of righteousness.*

> *Put your hope in the LORD,*
> *for with the LORD is unfailing love.*
>
> PSALM 130:7

Scripture references (in order of starred references in prayer):
1 Corinthians 15:33; 1 Thessalonians 4:9–10; 2 Peter 3:9;
1 Corinthians 15:58; Proverbs 27:17; Psalm 23:3

My prayer for my teen today:

The character trait of God that I will focus on today:
(Thank you, God, that you are . . .)

One promise of Scripture for today:

Loneliness

We can't fix things for our teens the way we could when they were little. We see our teen's loneliness but can do nothing. We can't make others reach out to him. We can't create friends for him. What can we do?

Father, my heart is breaking as I watch my son's heart break. He doesn't say much. His silence comes from a pain that cannot be spoken. His pain may not be obvious to others, but I can feel his loneliness. He watches the other guys in the "in crowd," guys with plenty of friends, full calendars, too much to do on weekends. Yet he sits alone.

Father, my heart aches for his loneliness. I don't understand why he has no friends. Have I done something wrong? Is it his personality? How can I help? What should I do?

Lord, I can come to you on his behalf. You understand loneliness. You felt it when your friends deserted you in the Garden of Gethsemane. You know his pain in a way I cannot. And you will comfort him.

I ask you to turn his darkness into light.* Give him the skills to be a friend and the courage to reach out to someone.* Lead him to your choice of a friend. I pray for that potential friend today. I ask you that he would be receptive to my son and that they would become companions together in their walk with you.

In this time of loneliness, show him that you want to be his friend. Reassure him of your own love toward him—love that no one can take away.* Reveal to him that you will never leave him.* Remind him that you hear when he calls to you and that you will answer him, lead him, and satisfy him.*

Great is our Lord and mighty in power;
his understanding has no limit.

PSALM 147:5

Scripture references (in order of starred references in prayer):
2 Samuel 22:29; Joshua 1:9; Romans 8:38–39; Hebrews 13:5b; Psalm 107:6–9

My prayer for my teen today:

The character trait of God that I will focus on today:
(Thank you, God, that you are . . .)

One promise of Scripture for today:

37

In a Hard Place

Life isn't fair. No one ever promised it would be. Bad things happen to good people. And when it's our teen who's hurt, our pain is doubled, for we hurt for our child and for ourselves as well. How do we handle this pain? Where do we find help?

Father, my child is in a hard place. And he hasn't really done anything wrong. All the things that have happened to him lately aren't his fault. Yes, I know we all play a part—but the rejection, the accident, the invitation that never came, the lousy grade he got on that test (and Lord, you know he really studied for this one), that person he can't please no matter how hard he tries, and those other things. . . . It seems so unfair. Life's tough for him right now.

Father, I hurt for my child. It pains me that I can't fix things for him. I long for someone to understand my pain and his!

God, you understand how painful this is for both of us. You care when your children hurt; your own son experienced pain on earth. Jesus, when you taught in Nazareth, your own hometown, people were so offended that they tried to throw you over a cliff.* You definitely did not win "speaker of the year"! You wept when your good friend Lazarus died.* You suffered abuse when you were beaten by a bunch of bullies before they crucified you.* And you didn't do anything wrong. You were sinless! While all this was happening to you, your Father in heaven was watching. You understand. He understands!

O Father, I pray that you would comfort my son. Help him to see that these trials are not a surprise or something strange but that you are in them.* Help him to see that this time of testing will develop perseverance and will help him become mature.* Reassure him that this sad time won't last forever; joy will come again!*

Father, help me to release him to you and to point him to you. Use this hard time to wean him from going to his parents for comfort that is inadequate, and instead teach him to turn to you for comfort that is supernatural and abundant.* And Father, in this process I too need to see your work in my teen's life apart from me.

Praise be to the God and Father of our Lord Jesus Christ, the Father of compassion and the God of all comfort, who comforts us in all our troubles, so that we can comfort those in any trouble with the comfort we ourselves have received from God.

2 CORINTHIANS 1:3–4

Scripture references (in order of starred references in prayer): Luke 4:28–30; John 11:35; Matthew 27:26; 1 Peter 4:12; James 1:2–5; Psalm 30:5b; Isaiah 49:13

My prayer for my teen today:

The character trait of God that I will focus on today:
(Thank you, God, that you are . . .)

One promise of Scripture for today:

Facing Temptation

Because we've been down the road ourselves, we more easily see the sign that blinks "Danger Ahead!" on a path that our child is traveling. But our teen doesn't seem to see it. Or if she does, she chooses to ignore it. Who will rescue her from the traps ahead?

God, today I am fearful. My teen is walking down a scary path, a path of temptation. She's being pulled in directions that are unhealthy (eating disorder, witchcraft, pornography, drugs, drinking, sex, materialism, depression, bad company, thrill of violence . . .). I don't know what she will do. I don't know if she will even think about the consequences of what she is doing or if she even sees where she is headed. And Father, even if she did recognize, even a little bit, what she's doing, I don't know if she would have the power to resist the temptation. I don't know if she'd want to resist it!

I can only imagine where she is going. My vision is flawed. I am so thankful, Father, that you see where she is headed.* Nothing is hidden from you.* In you is light and no darkness

41

at all.* Father, open her eyes.* Show her the dangerous path that she is considering. Make her miserable with her direction.* Woo her back to you, O Lord. Remind her that your plan for her is far better than anything the world offers.

Reveal to her that you are far more powerful than the enemy.* Please show her that she can resist temptation if she calls on you, for you have promised that with every temptation you will provide a means of escape for those who choose to take it.*

Father, today I ask you to rescue her and provide her with a means of escape.

*Rescue me and deliver me in your righteousness;
turn your ear to me and save me.*

PSALM 71:2

Scripture references (in order of starred references in prayer): Proverbs 15:3; Psalm 139:7–10; 1 John 1:5; Psalm 119:18; John 16:8; 1 John 4:4; 1 Corinthians 10:13

My prayer for my teen today:

The character trait of God that I will focus on today: (Thank you, God, that you are . . .)

One promise of Scripture for today:

A Rebellious Teen

We may be struggling with a rebellious child. That very child we tried so hard to raise right is now alienated from us. Asking "why?" causes pain, and figuring out what to do is not easy. We need divine intervention! (If your child isn't in this situation, you probably know a grieving parent who does have a child like this. Use this prayer to pray for her child. Pray especially that God would comfort her and give her hope. Part of being the body of Christ involves carrying one another's burdens. Today you can be a "burden-carrier" for another parent.)

Father, why do I have such a rebellious child? He's chosen to go his own way, and he's cut us off. He's not only estranged himself from us but alienated his siblings as well. He seems determined to go against everything we've tried to teach him.

He refuses to talk with us. He doesn't want to be around us. It's as if he's rejected his family and replaced us with people who are immoral, unhealthy, and dangerous. He's hiding from you, O Lord. Nothing we try works, and it seems there's nothing left to do. We are at the end of our resources.

In this mess, it's easy for me to wallow in guilt and to wonder where we went wrong. It's easy to blame my spouse. It's easy to dwell on the "if onlys"—If only we hadn't . . . or we had . . . , If only he wasn't . . ." Father, deliver me from wallowing in self-pity. Keep me from blaming others. Do not let the enemy use this to divide us in our marriage.* Instead draw us closer to each other.*

Father, thank you that although my child hides, he is not hidden from you.* You see him and you have your hand on him.* He is in a real pit, but you long to redeem him from this pit!* You want to bring him back. You are his redeemer.* You can restore him!* Lord, I want to believe all this, but it's hard. Help me overcome my unbelief!* Help me trust you with my child.

For nothing is impossible with God.

LUKE 1:37

Scripture references (in order of starred references in prayer): 1 Peter 5:8–9; James 4:7–10; Jeremiah 23:23–24; Psalm 37:23–24; Psalm 103:4; Isaiah 43:1; Jeremiah 32:26–27; Mark 9:24

My prayer for my teen today:

44

The character trait of God that I will focus on today:
(Thank you, God, that you are . . .)

One promise of Scripture for today:

Role Models

During these teen years we become more aware than ever before of the importance of good role models for our child. She needs mentors whom she can look up to. She isn't as willing to hear things from us parents. She's more likely to listen to other people, especially "cool" folks a few years older than she is. Or even adults who take an interest in her.

I can't raise this teen by myself. She doesn't want to hear things from me. I need help. I need support. I long for someone else to "take her on," and she needs someone other than her parent!

Too often I try to be everything for her. I think I should be able to. After all, I'm her parent! But I can't, Lord. I am so relieved that I'm not supposed to. This is an example of how much we need each other in the body of Christ.*

Father, I ask you to send into my teen's life one or two

sharp older friends. Give her older friends who love you and who will reach out to her.* Father, she needs some same-sex mentors who can really challenge her, and she needs opposite-sex mentors who can set a high standard as she looks for a future mate.* I pray that these mentors would love your Word and seek to follow it.* I pray for that potential mentor today that you would touch her heart and nudge her to seek out my child. And Lord, show me how I can continue to pray for this mentor as she cares for my teen.*

Even as an adult I recognize that I too benefit from the wisdom of older mentors. And I realize that I need to be available to be that older mentor in a young person's life. Make me willing to be the answer to the prayers of another parent who is praying for a mentor for their child. Show me a teen whom I can care for.*

The LORD will hear when I call to him.

PSALM 4:3

Scripture references (in order of starred references in prayer): Ephesians 4:16; John 17:20–21; Proverbs 27:17; John 17:17; Philemon 4–7; Titus 2:3 and Ephesians 4:16

My prayer for my teen today:

47

The character trait of God that I will focus on today:
(Thank you, God, that you are . . .)

One promise of Scripture for today:

Decision Making

Decision making is one of the toughest challenges in life. It's doubly tough when we have a teen because that teen needs to learn to make his own decisions. We may not trust his discernment. And we may not know the right answer either! Yet learning to make decisions is crucial to maturity.

Father, my son has an important decision to make. He doesn't know which way to go! There are so many ways to look at this, so many factors to consider, so many unknowns. Nothing is clear. It's overwhelming.

I don't know what is right either. When he was small, I knew how to make decisions that were best for him. But now I don't, and it's frustrating. And this decision is really important. It could impact the rest of his life.

Perhaps, Father, you have hidden the right decision from me because you are going to show him. It's time for me to be weaned from some of my parenting responsibilities and begin to trust you to work in my child's life without me. This is new for me, O Lord, and it's scary.

Thank you, Lord, that I can have the confidence that you are at work in my son's life.* Thank you that you want him to know your will far more than either he or I want to!* Give him the power to discern what is best.* Speak directly to him and show him what your will is in this matter.*

Father, in this process help me to take a fresh step in trusting you in new ways with my child. Thank you that this is not just for him. It's for me too. Give me eyes to see the specific lessons you have in this for me. Reveal to me a deeper aspect of your love and your sovereignty.

May the God of peace, who through the blood of the eternal covenant brought back from the dead our Lord Jesus, that great Shepherd of the sheep, equip you with everything good for doing his will, and may he work in us what is pleasing to him, through Jesus Christ, to whom be glory for ever and ever. Amen.

HEBREWS 13:20–21

Scripture references (in order of starred references in prayer): Philippians 1:6 and 2:13; Philippians 1:9–11; Psalm 25:12, 14 and Jeremiah 42:3; Proverbs 3:5–7

My prayer for my teen today:

The character trait of God that I will focus on today:
(Thank you, God, that you are . . .)

One promise of Scripture for today:

From Self-Centered to Other-Centered

We all grow weary of a teen who can't be satisfied. From her perspective, there's never enough, or it's never right. Her focus seems to be, "Make me happy, cater to me." But as parents we can't, and we shouldn't. So what do we do?

Father, this teenage season is so "me-centered." Satisfy me, meet my needs, make me happy, entertain me, please me. I know this is part of our sin nature. I'm that way too—but Lord, this selfishness sure seems magnified in teenagers! It's so easy for my teen to be in a bad mood when things don't go the way she wants. Some days her world seems to revolve around her, and that world is way too small. I long for my child to develop into an adult who is more "other-centered" than "me-centered."

Father, you long for this too. In your greatest commandment, you called us to love you with all our heart, mind, and soul and to love our neighbors as ourselves.* You demonstrated this when you gave your only Son for us!* You are a giving God. You gave freely without expectation of anything in return (and what you got in return was horrible rejection). Your nature is perfectly, lovingly "other-centered."

Your apostle Paul reminds us not to think of ourselves more highly than we ought* (or more frequently than we ought!) and to do nothing out of selfish ambition or vain conceit but in humility to consider others better than ourselves.*

Father, this is hard; it's not natural, but I pray that my teen would begin to notice other people and ask, What are her needs? How can I care for her? Give my child eyes to notice the lonely, the wounded, the unattractive in her classes, at lunch, and on the athletic field and ask, How can I care for that person? Show her ways to act with love (by a compliment, a kind word, an invitation to eat lunch together, etc.). Show me some specific ways that we can begin to do this more as a family.

The Counselor, the Holy Spirit, whom the Father will send in my name, will teach you all things and will remind you of everything I have said to you.

JOHN 14:26

Scripture references (in order of starred references in prayer): Matthew 22:37–39; John 3:16; Romans 12:3; Philippians 2:3–4

My prayer for my teen today:

53

The character trait of God that I will focus on today:
(Thank you, God, that you are . . .)

One promise of Scripture for today:

From Failure to Forgiveness

You and I are going to fail. It's a given. Human nature means we are prone to cheat, lie, or behave immorally in countless ways. Our teens are also going to fail. Failure is a very real part of life. But it need not be devastating. It can be redemptive. How do we handle it when our teen fails?

Lord, my child has failed. He knows he's let us down. He's let other people down, and most of all he's let you down. He knows that he's done what he ought not to have done. He's mad at himself, and he's embarrassed. He's very sad. He has already suffered some of the consequences of his actions.

Father, I'm so grateful for his tender conscience. Yes, it causes great pain, but it calls forth repentance. Thank you for protecting him from hardness of heart. In his agony bring him to full repentance. Protect him from self-justification. Help him to know that it is a broken and contrite heart that you will not despise!* Help him to see that with you there is complete forgiveness.* Show him that you are not shocked by what he's done, for you know our hearts.* You know how very fragile we are.*

King David was a man after your own heart, yet he lied, he committed adultery, he even committed murder, and still you forgave him. When you forgive, O Lord, you cast our sins as far as the east is from the west and remember them no more.*

Father, as a result of what's happened, my son could so easily live in a prison of self-condemnation. I ask you not to let this happen but to enable him to experience the amazing joy of knowing that there is now no condemnation for those in Christ Jesus.* Help him to feel truly clean. Fill him with the assurance of forgiveness!

Therefore, there is now no condemnation for those who are in Christ Jesus, because through Christ Jesus the law of the Spirit of life set me free from the law of sin and death.

ROMANS 8:1–2

Scripture references (in order of starred references in prayer):
Psalm 51:17; Psalm 130:3–4; 1 Chronicles 28:9; Psalm 103:13–14; Psalm 103:12; Romans 8:1–2

My prayer for my teen today:

The character trait of God that I will focus on today:
(Thank you, God, that you are . . .)

One promise of Scripture for today:

A Questioning Faith

The teen years are years of questioning for our child. This includes questions about the faith: "Why should I believe what my parents have taught me?" "Is it true?" "Do I want to believe it?" It's a hard time for us, the parents, and a necessary yet difficult time for our child.

Father, these teen years are unsettling in terms of my child's faith. I know she knows your truth. She's certainly heard it from me for ages. Yet I don't know what she thinks deep in her heart. This is a season of questioning for her on so many fronts, and that seems to include her faith. It's hard because I'm sure she wonders if she can believe what she has been taught. She probably wonders if she even wants to.

It's hard for me too, O Lord, because her walk with you is the most important thing to me. Yet I sense that I am limited in what I can do to help. I can expose her to strong youth ministries and godly role models. I can pray. But I can't convince her. Only you can do that.*

You, O Lord, are the one who began the work in her. You will complete it.* You are the one who will keep her strong. You are the one who is faithful.*

Father, I pray that you would bring her through these teen years more convinced of you and more determined to walk with you no matter the cost. I pray that she would move from an inherited faith to a deeply personal faith. She cannot live on an inherited faith; belief has to be hers personally. Bring her to the place of owning her faith.*

I pray also that the eyes of your heart may be enlightened in order that you may know the hope to which he has called you, the riches of his glorious inheritance in the saints, and his incomparably great power for us who believe.

EPHESIANS 1:18–19

Scripture references (in order of starred references in prayer): John 6:44; Philippians 1:6; 1 Corinthians 1:8–9; Psalm 78:1–8

My prayer for my teen today:

The character trait of God that I will focus on today: (Thank you, God, that you are . . .)

One promise of Scripture for today:

Sibling Rivalry

As parents we often feel like we've spent our whole life battling sibling rivalry. Perhaps we thought we were making headway. And then we had teenagers! Now, once again, our home seems to be more of a battlefront than a place of refuge. How do we handle this?

Father, these teen years are so hard on sibling relationships! I thought I was past those long years of sibling rivalry—those years of hitting, biting, nasty words, and temper tantrums. For a while it even seemed like they were beginning to get along, and I got my hopes up. But now, O Lord, it's back. And it's more subtle and in a way nastier. Their mood swings don't help. Their ugly words seem to hurt more. Self-image is so fragile. It's so easy to be misunderstood. I thought I'd taught them kindness and thoughtfulness and respect. But now . . .

Lord, you understand how I feel. Surely your heart was broken when your own disciples got into an argument about who was the greatest.* You had spent nearly three years teaching them, and they still argued like siblings. And they even had you! You understand why I feel like a failure as a parent. You have felt not only this but all of my feelings. You too have suffered as a parent suffers. Your disciples were like your children. Even though you never sinned, you still had to experience all the disappointments and hurts that I will experience.*

Thank you, Father, that I can come to you, the only one who truly understands. You love my children even more than I do. You know them better than I do.* You want them to love each other.* I pray that they will come through this time and grow into siblings who truly love each other. I long for them to be intentional in caring for each other, to become friends as adults. Father, show me what I need to do to continue training them in this. Show me how to discipline and how to teach them to encourage each other.

Thank you for your comfort. Now I need your wisdom.*

For this reason he had to be made like his brothers in every way, in order that he might become a merciful and faithful high priest in service to God, and that he might make atonement for the sins of the people. Because he himself suffered when he was tempted, he is able to help those who are being tempted.

HEBREWS 2:17–18, EMPHASIS ADDED

Scripture references (in order of starred references in prayer):
Mark 9:33–34 and Luke 22:24; Hebrews 2:17–18 and 4:14–16; Psalm 139:1–4; John 13:34–35; James 1:5

61

My prayer for my teen today:

The character trait of God that I will focus on today:
(Thank you, God, that you are . . .)

One promise of Scripture for today:

Setting Limits and Letting Go

So often it seems that every issue with our teen turns into a major debate. Things aren't as black-and-white as they were when she was little. It was so much simpler when she was two and threw a temper tantrum. Then we won the battle. Now her arguments are so much smarter. How do I set limits and yet let go at the same time?

Lord, today I'm hearing, "Why can't you trust me? You just don't understand. Everyone else gets to . . ."

Lord, she's right. I don't always trust her, because she doesn't have the wisdom or experience yet. I don't understand everything. And yes, some of her friends get to. . . . But I'm not her friend's parent, I'm hers. And she is my responsibility. You have given her to me to raise. (Sometimes I wonder if you were thinking clearly when you did that, Lord!) I know I have to set limits and yet begin to let go. It's so hard. She doesn't like me at these times. I know I'm not running for the most popular parent in town. But today, I feel like the worst! I realize that I have to remember that what she thinks of me now is not nearly as important as what she'll think of me ten years from now. Even C. S. Lewis said, "Being brought up, no matter how graciously done, is bound to offend."

Father, you have given me this particular child. You have promised that you will give me what I need to raise her.* Lord, I know she will be more likely to want to obey you if I have taught her to obey me. The love and hugs I give her are important, but you love her even more than I do.* Please show me the areas in which I need to be firm and the areas in which I need to begin to let go.* Thank you that love and discipline are not opposites but partners and that even though discipline is painful at the moment, it is for our own good and will result in righteousness and peace.*

No discipline seems pleasant at the time, but painful. Later on, however, it produces a harvest of righteousness and peace for those who have been trained by it.

HEBREWS 12:11

Scripture references (in order of starred references in prayer): 1 Thessalonians 5:24; Exodus 34:6; Proverbs 19:18 and 23:12; Hebrews 12:11

My prayer for my teen today:

The character trait of God that I will focus on today:
(Thank you, God, that you are . . .)

One promise of Scripture for today:

Driving

I should be excited for my teen. He's about to get his driver's license! For him it's a rite of passage, but to me it's a responsibility. I'm not sure he's ready! (I still remember those stunts on his bicycle!) And I'm not at all sure that I am ready either! How do I handle these conflicting emotions?

Lord, my child is about to get his driver's license. This is so frightening for me. I know in the scheme of world affairs this isn't a big deal. I'm almost embarrassed to mention it to you when so many parents have much bigger issues. I guess I should be thankful it's only a car. But I'm scared!

He could so easily have an accident. He's inexperienced. He might get distracted by friends in the car or cell phones or music or fast food. I'm not sure he has the judgment necessary for this responsibility. Does he realize the car can be a dangerous weapon? And then there are the other drivers. What if one comes toward him? What if he gets hit? His reactions aren't fine tuned yet. He might not be able to avoid an oncoming car or deer or careless pedestrian. What if he's tempted to drink? What if he's overcome by road rage—his own or others'?

Lord, I cannot dwell in the "what ifs." You have promised to give me faith for today.* One day at a time. Father, I know I have to let him go and trust you in a new way. I cannot protect him.* I ask you to surround the car with your angels and to protect him from all harm.* Help me to see that you will use this to grow me up in trusting you in new ways as I have to let go. Help me realize again that you are faithful.*

Give us wisdom as we write out specific guidelines for his driving.* Guide our conversation as we discuss this with him. Father, it's easy for this to be "heavy." Instead help us to rejoice in this occasion with him as a part of his maturing. Show me a specific way our family can celebrate this milestone for him!

You are my hiding place;
you will protect me from trouble
and surround me with songs of deliverance.

PSALM 32:7

Scripture references (in order of starred references in prayer):
Matthew 6:11, 34; John 17:11; Hebrews 1:14 and Psalm 91:11; Deuteronomy 7:9; James 1:5

My prayer for my teen today:

The character trait of God that I will focus on today:
(Thank you, God, that you are . . .)

One promise of Scripture for today:

Note: A helpful driving contract for you to use with your teen can be found in Appendix 2.

Waiting

Y ou'll just have to wait." I hate that phrase. Nothing in me likes to wait. I want answers now. I want guidance now. I want things to be fixed now. I don't like the pain of waiting. And I really feel helpless when I have to wait on God, especially when it comes to my child.

O Lord, today I feel stuck. I can't hear you. I don't know the answers. I don't know what to do, and I feel helpless. I want to help my child, but I don't know how.

Where are you, O Lord? Don't you hear me? Don't you care?

I feel like I'm "on hold." I'm calling to you, but I can't hear your answers. What is going on? Could it be that I have to learn to wait? Could it be that my teen has to learn to wait? I don't like to wait, Father. I live in an instant society. I expect you to work instantly too. I know that a lot of life is waiting, but it's so hard. It hurts to watch my child suffer. What if she thinks you don't care?

But you do care, O Lord.* It's good for my child to learn to wait while she's young.* She will have to wait on things when she's an adult, so this is good preparation.

In the waiting you have something special to teach her and to teach me. Give each of us ears to hear what you would say in this time of waiting. Show us new things about you.* I think of how you waited, sending Jesus in the fullness of time.* Thank you that you do what is best and not necessarily what is fast. Thank you that you are working even when I can't see it, and O Lord, right now I can't see it.

Help me to know how to explain the "benefits of learning to wait" to her. Enable the two of us to communicate at a deeper level than we ever have before. Show each of us something that we can share to encourage each other. Make this a faith-building time in her life and in mine.

Bring us through this season of waiting with a fresh sense of your presence. Thank you for promising that you can use everything—even waiting—for good in our lives.*

Call to me and I will answer you, and will tell you great and hidden things that you have not known.

JEREMIAH 33:3 ESV

Scripture references (in order of starred references in prayer): Isaiah 30:18; Psalm 27:14 and Isaiah 40:30–31; Jeremiah 33:3; Galatians 4:4; Romans 8:28

My prayer for my teen today:

The character trait of God that I will focus on today:
(Thank you, God, that you are . . .)

One promise of Scripture for today:

Integrity

Very few people in today's world seem to applaud integrity. Turn on the news and you will see another story of an athlete who has used performance-enhancing drugs or a corporate executive who has manipulated financial records. Yet we know that integrity is the cornerstone of all values. How do we teach our teens the value of honesty in a world of compromise? How do I grow in this myself?

Father, being a person of integrity is so hard in today's culture. Our world screams, "It doesn't matter what you do as long as no one gets hurt and no one finds out." But God, your standard is *to do what's right when no one is looking and no one will find out*. I feel like your standard gets buried in the pressures of today. My teen is hit with this all day long! Cheating just a little bit, lying just a little, misrepresenting the facts, shading the truth, deceiving adults and friends in his life. And all the time, rationalizing that it's okay, it's just a little thing.

But it's not okay. Father, you have called us to be people of complete integrity. You have told us that integrity gives us security.* That being dishonest will ultimately lead to downfall.* You have called us to be speakers of the truth.*

O God, you know it's not just my teen. It's me too. I don't always tell the complete truth. Too often I think the end will justify the means. And I know that's wrong. Forgive me, Lord. Make me like Job, who in the midst of horrible circumstances and loss and temptation determined to maintain his integrity until death.*

Father, I ask today that if my teen is doing anything dishonest, he will get caught. Show him the ultimate consequences of dishonesty while he's young. And when he's caught, help me to let him suffer the consequences of his actions and not bail him out. Help us to see this as a good lesson in the value of integrity. Reveal to us the subtleties of deceit. Keep us from becoming numbed by deception, and instead make us sensitive to your whispers. Guide us in your truth.*

When he, the Spirit of truth, comes, he will guide you into all truth.

JOHN 16:13

Scripture references (in order of starred references in prayer): Proverbs 10:9; Proverbs 11:3; Zechariah 8:16–17; Job 27:5–6; Psalm 25:5

My prayer for my teen today:

The character trait of God that I will focus on today:
(Thank you, God, that you are . . .)

One promise of Scripture for today:

An Angry Teen

Anger management. Is that really possible? Should a believer be angry? How do we handle anger? What do I do with an angry teenager?

Father, my teen is so angry, and I'm so exhausted. I fluctuate between anger, hurt, and guilt myself. When she said to me, "You weren't there for me when I needed you," it really stung. She's so angry at the many things that have happened to her. (Of course she thinks nothing is her fault!) She's quick to blame one of her parents, her siblings, her friends, or her circumstances for her misery and her behavior. And yes, Lord, in some ways she's right. I have failed. Some of her anger is justified. But Lord, I know that doesn't give her the right to behave in such anger, to wallow in the "victim trap" so popular in today's culture.

Father, thank you that you understand anger. You got angry yourself with the children of Israel when they turned to other gods.* And your Son Jesus got so angry with the money changers in the temple that he threw them out!* Anger in itself isn't wrong. But when it turns into bitterness, self-pity, or a justification for wrong behavior and bad attitudes, it is sin.*

Thank you that you are slow to anger and quick to forgive.* Thank you that you have forgiven me for the ways I've let my child down.* Thank you that you do not condemn me at all.* Thank you that I do not have to live one minute longer with a burden of guilt. Yes, I have sorrow, but in your time you will wipe away those tears.*

Father, please help my teen come to understand that she is responsible for her attitude. When she's angry, teach her to come quickly to you, to lay her anger at your feet and refuse to nurse its growth. Show her that she will only experience true freedom as she forgives, quits blaming, and moves on. Put people in her life who will reinforce this. Wash over her with the freedom that comes with repentance and forgiveness.*

The LORD, the compassionate and gracious God, slow to anger, abounding in love and faithfulness, maintaining love to thousands, and forgiving wickedness, rebellion and sin.

EXODUS 34:6–7

Scripture references (in order of starred references in prayer): Deuteronomy 29:26–28; Mark 11:12–17; Proverbs 29:11; 1 Corinthians 13:5; 1 John 1:9; Romans 8:1–2; Revelation 7:17; Psalm 32:1–5

My prayer for my teen today:

The character trait of God that I will focus on today:
(Thank you, God, that you are . . .)

One promise of Scripture for today:

Wisdom to Prioritize

My calendar is too full. I live with the illusion that "life will calm down." It will not. It will only become more complicated. My teen has the same problem. There are too many options for her. How should she spend her time? How can I guide her when I have the same problem?

Father, life is so full, too full. My teen could spend her time so many ways. Those extra classes, sports, music groups, church, special opportunities—and then there are friends, family, and chores! I know she's feeling overwhelmed because I am. It wouldn't be so difficult if the choices were between good and bad. But there are too many good choices. And as options continue to increase, it's going to get harder, not easier, to make wise choices. How does she decide? Where do we find priorities? How do I give her guidance when I have the same problem in my own life?

Thank you, Father, that you haven't sent us into this world and expected us to guess how to live. You've given us priorities for living, whether in a complex environment or a simple one. You've taught us that our first priority is to love you and our second one is to love our neighbor.* You have also shown us that life has seasons. We can't "do it all" in any one season.* Sometimes we have to learn to postpone to a later season some things we'd like to do now.

Father, thank you that you care about the little things like which sport to concentrate on, whether to take that advanced class, if working part-time makes sense, if a certain club is the right one.*

Father, today I ask you to give her your wisdom as she decides what to say "yes" to, what to say "no" to, and what to postpone.* Help her to seek you first for guidance and to make her first priority spending time alone with you each day.*

She has to make some hard choices. In the midst of her choices, I have to protect family time, and that isn't easy to do with a teen. Yet I know that ten years from now it will be more important that we said "no" to one more activity that lasts a season and instead ate dinner together to nurture family friendships that will last a lifetime. Give us a long-range perspective as we make these choices. Show us your wisdom.*

I love the LORD, for he heard my voice;
he heard my cry for mercy.
Because he turned his ear to me,
I will call on him as long as I live.

PSALM 116:1–2

Scripture references (in order of starred references in prayer):
Matthew 22:37; Ecclesiastes 3:1; Matthew 6:26; James 1:5;
Matthew 6:33; James 3:17–18

My prayer for my teen today:

The character trait of God that I will focus on today:
(Thank you, God, that you are . . .)

One promise of Scripture for today:

Tongue Control

Back talk, rudeness, unacceptable language—and all in my home! Sometimes it's subtle, often it's "in your face." I know this is not right. It hurts. Sometimes I react angrily myself. I don't want my home to be the scene of a verbal sword fight. How can I deal with a teenager who is using words in this way?

Father, my child has a "mouth." And it isn't always nice. In fact, it can be nasty. He can't seem to control his tongue. It's so easy for him to hurt others without realizing what he is doing. I wish I could tape-record him and play it back to him at the right moment so he could hear how he comes across!

Father, you aren't surprised at the evil that comes out of his mouth. (And yes, Lord, sometimes from my mouth too.) You have written so much in your Scriptures about our tongue! You have compared its power to that of a forest fire.* You have warned us to keep a rein on it, to keep it from speaking evil.* You have also called us to use it to bless others, even those who hurt us.* That is hard, Lord.

Father, I ask that you would teach my son to tame his tongue (and me to tame mine!). Lord, I hope I'm raising a future husband and father. I don't want him to one day verbally abuse his own wife or kids. He must learn to control his tongue now. Give him the discipline to keep his mouth shut when he should.* Convict him of verbal abuse as it occurs. Make him miserable and repentant. Cause him to turn to you for help, and when he does, let him see progress! He needs your encouragement.

Show him how to begin to use his tongue in a positive way. Make him a better affirmer of people. Teach him how to compliment and to appreciate other people.* Show me specific ways in which I can help him learn how to build others up. And Father, please control my own tongue today. Put new words in my mouth and in my son's mouth.

I waited patiently for the LORD;
he turned to me and heard my cry.
He lifted me out of the slimy pit,
out of the mud and mire;
he set my feet on a rock
and gave me a firm place to stand.
He put a new song in my mouth,
a hymn of praise to our God.
Many will see and fear
and put their trust in the LORD.

PSALM 40:1–3

Scripture references (in order of starred references in prayer):
James 3:5–6; James 1:26; Romans 12:14; Proverbs 11:12;
1 Peter 3:8–9

My prayer for my teen today:

The character trait of God that I will focus on today:
(Thank you, God, that you are . . .)

One promise of Scripture for today:

Courage

Where is a person who will stand strong? Who will do what is right no matter what the consequences might be? I long for that to be my teen. I too long for that sort of courage.

Father, today I'm thinking about courage. How I long for my son to become a man of courage. In this post-9/11 world it can be hard. He's growing up in a world of terrorists and in a world of confusion. Truth has become relative. Marriage is being redefined. The distinction between right and wrong has become blurred.

He's under pressure at school to be politically correct, to offend no one. Tolerance has become an idol. If one is tolerant, one accepts anything. "Acceptance" can mean going along with the crowd, or at least keeping his mouth shut if he disagrees with the crowd. Even if the crowd is very, very wrong. Sometimes the crowd isn't only his peers; it's the adults too.

I see the same thing in my own life, Father. It's so much easier for me to just go along with other adults than it is to take a stand and risk being thought foolish.

Father, you haven't called us to go along or to remain silent. You have called us to speak the truth in love.* Your desire is that we engage the culture, not withdraw from it.* But that takes courage.

Father, throughout history those who follow you have been in the minority. Yet you have given them the strength and the courage to stand strong. I pray that you would give my son clear convictions and the courage to stand firm. Give him the strength to resist the pressure to join the crowd when they do things they shouldn't. Give him wisdom to discern the crowd's false messages and instead to proclaim the truth with grace. And Father, I ask for these things for myself as well.

Make my son bold and thoughtful in engaging the culture.* Give him the courage to speak out with your truth. Lord, at times he will have to stand alone. Give him an overwhelming sense of your presence when this happens. Remind him that others may desert him but you never will.* Thank you that you honor and use men and women of courage.

Be strong and courageous. Do not be terrified; do not be discouraged, for the LORD your God will be with you wherever you go.

JOSHUA 1:9

Scripture references (in order of starred references in prayer): Ephesians 4:15; Ephesians 6:14–15 and Acts 1:8; Psalm 138:3; Hebrews 13:5b

My prayer for my teen today:

The character trait of God that I will focus on today:
(Thank you, God, that you are . . .)

One promise of Scripture for today:

A New School

The decision to choose a new school can give a parent ulcers. It can cause dissension in a marriage. We may have different perspectives. There are either too many options or not enough. After the decision is made, uncertainty still remains. Our child has to enter the new school. And new adjustments are waiting.

O Father, my child is about to enter a new school. This has not been an easy decision to make. You know how we have anguished over it! Is this the right place for her? Will the academic environment be what she needs to excel without being overwhelmed? Will she find friends with good values, friends who will encourage her in her faith, or friends who will ridicule her for her faith? Will she be drawn into a healthy group or enticed by a wild crowd? Will anyone reach out to her?

These changes are so frightening because the stakes are so high. Her college choice could be determined by this selection. Her friendships will be influenced by this change. Our relationship with her is going to be impacted by this decision we have made. She may be angry with us. And there are no guarantees that we have made the right choice. We can't see the future.*

Father, we need your perspective. You are so much bigger than this decision. You know our hearts. We want what is right for our child, and we've done our best to seek your will. If we are making a mistake, please overrule it.* You have promised that you will use anything for good in our lives and in her life, even our mistakes.*

At this moment I choose to thank you that you are in charge. You know my child better than I do.* You are a "go-before-you" God who prepares the way.* I ask that you would prepare the right teachers for my child. I ask that you would give her close female friends, ones who will be a positive influence. Go before her and protect her from unhealthy choices.

Father, this is a risk for all of us because it's an unknown. But it's time. I have to trust you in a new way, and she must too. In this new venture, help her to realize that you are her Father, not merely mine. Help her to see in a fresh way that you do have a special plan for her life. Use this to draw her closer to you.

Trust in the LORD with all your heart
and lean not on your own understanding;
in all your ways acknowledge him,
and he will make your paths straight.

PROVERBS 3:5–6

Scripture references (in order of starred references in prayer): 2 Corinthians 5:7; Luke 1:37; Romans 8:28; Psalm 139:13–16; Ephesians 4:12

My prayer for my teen today:

The character trait of God that I will focus on today:
(Thank you, God, that you are . . .)

One promise of Scripture for today:

Cultivating Joy

Depression seems so prevalent all around us. Some people have chemical reasons for sickness, others are physical, yet most others simply fall into a malaise. Where is joy? Where is wholesome laughter?

Father, my teen so frequently feels down. I know introspection and insecurity are normal to some degree with teens, but today, depression seems all too accepted.

Circumstances too frequently control his disposition. He is often disappointed by unfulfilled expectations. He too easily could fall into a depressed state.

Father, you do not want him to live like this. You have given him your Holy Spirit to fill him with joy regardless of his circumstances.* Your Scriptures are full of stories about your people in difficult circumstances, still remaining joyful! I think of Shadrach, Meshach, and Abednego worshiping God as they prepared to die in the furnace.* Or of Nehemiah facing opposition as he led his people back to Jerusalem to rebuild their temple.* Or of Mary, the mother of Jesus, who, after she recovered from her shock and fear of hearing what you had chosen her to do, began to sing with joy.* Each of these people chose to trust you. And you filled them with joy.

Father, we can't churn up joy on our own. But we can choose to trust you and to ask you for joy. You have promised to give it to us!* Father, I ask that you would overwhelm my son with joy today. I pray also that you will give him friends who will make him laugh. We all need people in our lives who help us laugh. Laughter is your gift! It helps restore our perspective in all situations. And as I think ahead, O Lord, I pray that one day you'll give my son a wife who will make him laugh. He will need laughter in his marriage.

Show me this day how to make my home a home of laughter—not laughter caused by sarcasm, but laughter in response to the pure joy of knowing you.*

He brought me out into a spacious place;
he rescued me because he delighted in me.

PSALM 18:19

Scripture references (in order of starred references in prayer): Galatians 5:22; Daniel 3:16–18; Nehemiah 8:10; Luke 1:46–47; John 15:9–11; 1 Peter 1:8

My prayer for my teen today:

The character trait of God that I will focus on today:
(Thank you, God, that you are . . .)

One promise of Scripture for today:

A Hunger for Faith

One of the hardest places for Christian parents to trust God is for the faith of their child. Perhaps this is because it's so important to us. We long for their faith to become solid, yet we fear it won't happen. In our heads we know it isn't up to us, but in our hearts we wonder if there isn't something more we should be doing. It's a hard place to trust God.

Lord, the greatest desire of my life is that my teen would love you with all her heart and walk with you all her life. I can't make this happen. (But you know how hard I do try to make it happen! And I fail. Miserably.) Only you can do this. I ask that you would create a hunger in her heart to know you. It's so easy for her to hunger after other things: popularity, relationships, acceptance, accomplishments, success, satisfaction. The culture puts so much emphasis on "doing what makes me happy and making sure I'm feeling good about myself." But none of these things will satisfy her.*

93

I so easily feel responsible for her faith and try to make her hunger for you. But I can't. Father, help me to let go of this burden of responsibility. Remind me that she is your responsibility.

Today she's hungering for things that I don't know about. And she doesn't even recognize the hungers in her own heart. She can't. Only you truly know the depths of her heart and mine.* You know how fragile we are. You've said we're as fragile as dust.* You alone understand our weaknesses. And you do not condemn us for them. What a relief this is!*

Father, you want my child to walk with you even more than I do. You created her with a specific purpose.* You have your eyes on her.* You have engraved her name in the palm of your hand.* At this very moment your Son Jesus is sitting at your right hand praying for my child.* Now, as I picture the two of you together sharing love for my daughter, I am comforted!

Therefore he is able to save completely those who come to God through him, because he always lives to intercede for them.

HEBREWS 7:25, EMPHASIS ADDED

Scripture references (in order of starred references in prayer):
Matthew 6:33; 1 Chronicles 28:9 and Psalm 139:23; Psalm 103:14; Romans 8:1–2; Jeremiah 29:11–13; Psalm 17:8; Isaiah 49:16; Romans 8:34

My prayer for my teen today:

The character trait of God that I will focus on today:
(Thank you, God, that you are . . .)

One promise of Scripture for today:

Sexual Identity

The struggle with sexual identity in our culture is one of the most difficult adjustments for today's Christian parent. Most likely it is out of our realm of experience. But believers cannot bury their heads in the sand. It is a real problem, and because of the culture our kids are growing up in, many of them will be challenged to question their own identity. Is God shocked? No. Does he care? Yes.

Help, Father! Today's world is so different from my world as a teen. When I was a teen, my friends and I didn't spend time questioning our sexual identity. But today it's everywhere. My son can't escape the pressure to wonder, to question his maleness.

Much of culture says "gay is normal." You may be "born that way." You "can't help it."

But your Word says we are born male and female.

Father, you know my son has determined to walk with you.

He's committed to saving your gift of sex for one woman in marriage. Because he has not had many girlfriends and doesn't have tales to tell in the locker room, perhaps he's beginning to wonder about his sexual identity. All of this is fearful and confusing to him and to me. On the one hand he's ashamed that he would even question his identity. On the other hand it's real.

Father, I know that he doesn't need a panicky parent right now. He needs reassurance. I desperately need your wisdom to know how to react to this shocking revelation. Show me how to help him realize that the teen years are full of conflicting emotions and physical desires. It's normal for him to question his desires. It does not mean he's gay. It means he's a typical boy in a very confused, sex-crazed culture. Help him to see that everyone is tempted—some to the same sex, some to the opposite sex, some to pornography, and so on. Your Word says that Jesus himself was tempted in every way that we are, yet was without sin.* Temptation is not sin. We don't have to give into temptation. We are to recognize it as coming from the enemy and stand firm.* Being tempted does not determine our nature! God does!* What a relief!

Thank you for the apostle Paul's strong words that temptations are common but have no power over us. We always have an escape.*

Reassure my child that you made him for yourself. Remind him that you did not create us to desire the same sex or animals.* These desires come from the enemy. Instead, your plan is for celibacy or for sexual fulfillment in marriage between a man and a woman.* Convince him that he does not need to worry about his identity. It was your choice when you created him.

So God created man in his own image, in the image of God he created him; male and female he created them. God blessed them and said to them,

"Be fruitful and increase in number; fill the earth and subdue it."

GENESIS 1:27–28

Scripture references (in order of starred references in prayer):
Hebrews 4:15–16; 1 Peter 5:8–9; Psalm 139:13–15;
1 Corinthians 10:13; Romans 1:26–31; 1 Corinthians
7:1–10

My prayer for my teen today:

The character trait of God that I will focus on today:
(Thank you, God, that you are . . .)

One promise of Scripture for today:

My Inadequacy

et me tell you a secret: No parent feels that he or she has done the job of raising a teen right. Not one single one. No perfect formula for raising teens exists. *Thankfully, it's not about us. It's about an almighty, loving God* who chose to use an ill-equipped parent to raise his precious child.

Lord, I am so inadequate to raise this teen. What were you thinking when you made me the parent?

I don't know how to raise her. I don't have a clue how to handle this tough issue we are facing. I don't know what to say. I don't even know how I'm supposed to feel! (In some ways I'm more confused than my teen, and I'm the parent!) No matter what I do, it seems the wrong thing. No matter what I say, it doesn't come out right.

I can't raise this teen, Lord!

Could it be, Lord, that you are using my teen to remind

me just how inadequate I am? Could it be that my pride has reared its ugly head? Pride that says I should know how to raise this child. Or self-pity that says, I don't know how to do this, because after all, my background was . . .

Father, forgive my pride and my self-pity. They are sin.* Thank you that at this very moment, you forgive me. I am clean.* And thank you that you will continue to forgive me when I fall into pride or self-pity in the future. Thank you that you do not condemn me.* You understand my frailty.* I'm the one who forgets my frailty. I'm the one who tries to be God, to fix everyone. And I can't. That's your job.*

Thank you that your love for me is not dependent on my being a good parent or raising a great teenager who "turns out right." No, you love me simply because I belong to you. Period.

The LORD your God is with you,
  he is mighty to save.
He will take great delight in you,
  he will quiet you with his love,
  he will rejoice over you with singing.

ZEPHANIAH 3:17

Scripture references (in order of starred references in prayer): Proverbs 8:13; 1 John 1:9; Psalm 103:12 and Romans 8:1–2; Psalm 103:13–14; Philippians 2:13

My prayer for my teen today:

The character trait of God that I will focus on today:
(Thank you, God, that you are . . .)

One promise of Scripture for today:

A Final Encouragement

My husband and I had been on the road speaking daily for nearly three weeks, and now we were on the plane headed home. I was exhausted, drained in every way—spiritually, mentally, emotionally, and physically. I could not wait to fall asleep in my own bed and not have to speak to anyone. And I couldn't wait to see my kids.

As I thought about the kids, my heart turned to one child in particular. *How is this child really doing?* I wondered. *Is my child struggling? Is the concern I have had about this teen valid? What if there's a bigger problem than I've suspected? What if things are really wrong? What if . . . ?*

The more I thought about my teen, the more anxious I became. My stomach turned to knots. I felt ill. The claustrophobic closeness of our crowded overseas flight smothered me. My exhaustion began to act as a potent fertilizer for my parental fear.

I know, I thought, *I'll read the Scriptures. Surely God will have a word for me there.* Pulling my Bible out of my crammed briefcase, I began to read the book of Psalms, desperately looking for answers and for peace. The more I read, the more I "read into" what I read. And what I read into certain verses stimulated my overactive imagination into imagining the worst scenario for my teen. Finding no peace in the Scriptures, I began to pray. But the more I prayed, the more I worried. Finally, in complete frustration, I cried out to the Lord.

"Lord, nothing is working. Please help me. Please, I need you so much."

I did not hear an audible voice, but the following words came into my head with such forceful clarity and soothing gentleness that I had no doubt from whom they came.

"Remember me."

A supernatural peace settled my anxious heart. I realized that in my exhausted, vulnerable state, I had let a possible problem become greater than my almighty God. I had forgotten who he is.

How easy it is for us, as parents of teens, to forget who God is and to let our issues become blown way out of proportion. Indeed, to let our issues become greater than our God. No matter what we are going through or may encounter with our teen, we have to remember who the Lord is.

He is the King of Kings. He is still in charge. He is the one who knows our child better than we do and who loves our child far more than we are capable of. He is the God from whom nothing is hidden. He is the God who rescues, the God who redeems, the God who forgives, the God for whom nothing is impossible. We *can* entrust our children to him. *He is worthy of our trust.*

Remember him.

Finding the Confidence to Pray

Perhaps you have picked up this book because you know you should be praying for your teen. Or perhaps a friend has given it to you because they want to encourage you.

But let's be honest. You may be thinking, *I can't do this. After all, I have so much in my own life that isn't right. I don't even know if I really believe anyone will hear my prayer. I don't really know if I have faith myself, so how can I pray for my teen?*

You are not alone. At some point in life most people have had similar thoughts. We wonder if God really is there. We wonder if he does care. We even question if it is possible to have a relationship with him when our own lives fall so far short of how we think he expects us to live.

Perhaps we *hope* it is all true, and we *hope* we have a relationship with him. Yet, still, there is a glimmer of doubt.

I grew up in a Christian home. I can't remember a time that I didn't believe in God or in his Son Jesus. I tried to read my Bible, but it wasn't especially meaningful. I assumed that being a Christian meant being good. And I assumed that when I died, if I'd been just a little bit more good than bad, I'd get to go to heaven. When I was a college student, I met some sharp graduate students. One of them asked me, "Susan, are you a Christian?"

"Well," I responded (thinking this was a very odd question coming from a cute guy!), "I think I am. I hope I am."

My wise friend replied, "Susan, God doesn't want you to *think* you are or to *hope* that you are. He wants you to *know* that you are a believer."

He went on to tell me that God loved me and had a specific plan for my life. But I, like everyone else, was sinful (selfish) and separated from God. No one could be good enough for God. My good works would never get me "there." Yet God didn't leave me in this state. He sent his Son Jesus to die for my sins in order that I might be able to approach and to know God personally. Then my friend shared a promise from the Bible with me, one meant to be a picture of Christ standing at the door of our heart. It says,

> Here I am! I stand at the door and knock. If anyone hears my voice and opens the door, I will come in. . . .
>
> REVELATION 3:20

My friend asked me, "Susan, have you ever asked Christ to come into your life, to be your personal Savior?"

I realized that I had not. Instead, because of my background, I had been living on an inherited faith, the faith of my parents. I needed a personal faith.

My friend asked me if I would like to pray a prayer and ask Christ to come into my life. Although I didn't understand it all and this seemed a bit odd, I knew that this was something I needed and wanted to do. And so I did. My friend prayed out loud, and I followed silently, using his words, and asked Christ to come into my life.

For me it wasn't an emotional experience. It was simply moving from an inherited faith to a personal faith. For others this decision is emotional. We are all different, and God meets each of us in our own uniqueness.

My friend Barbara grew up in a scientific, agnostic home. Matters of faith were ridiculed and rarely discussed. She went into marriage and parenting with no religious background and no real interest in God. Yet as she and her husband encountered the challenges of the corporate world, marriage, and parenting, they realized they needed something. There had to be something more to life. There had to be a deeper purpose. There had to be help for them as they raised their kids. They began to look for God.

In time they too came to the place where they each asked Christ to come into their lives and to come into the heart of their family.

No matter what our background is or what we've done or not done, God longs for each of us to come to him just as we are. He wants us to have the certainty of knowing him personally, not simply a vague hope that he exists.

Friend, if you aren't sure that you've ever asked Christ into your heart and you would like to, please don't wait any longer. I'm going to share a prayer similar to the one that I prayed when I asked him to come into my heart. I would encourage you to pray this prayer for yourself and ask him to come into your heart.

Dear Lord, I need you. I open the door of my heart and ask you to come in. Thank you for dying on the cross for me. Thank you that this painful act of yours has allowed my sins to be forgiven. Thank you that you have promised that you will never leave me. Thank you that I can know right now that one day I'll be in heaven with you, not because I'm good but because I'm forgiven.

When you ask Christ to come into your heart, several things happen.

1. He comes in! You may or may not have experienced strong feelings when you prayed. If you did, that's wonderful. But if you didn't, don't worry. Feelings or lack of feelings don't determine Christ's coming into our lives. He comes in response to being asked. Our relationship with him is not based on our feelings. (What a relief!) It is based on faith in the fact that he will do what he has promised. See Revelation 3:20 and Titus 1:2.

2. He will never leave you. He promises that even when you forget him or mess up, he will never leave you. See Hebrews 13:5 and Psalm 139:7–10.

3. All your sins are forgiven. When you ask God to forgive your sins, he does. Yes, even that one you can barely admit. He has forgiven that one too. And he stands ready to forgive your future sins when you mess up. All you need to do is to confess them and ask for his forgiveness. See 1 John 1:9 and Psalm 103:12.

4. You can know that one day you will be in heaven with him. Going to heaven isn't dependent on being good. You could never be good enough. No one can. It is dependent on Christ taking your sins on his shoulders to the cross. See 1 John 5:11–12.

5. He has given you his Holy Spirit to give you the power to live the life he has planned for you to live. It isn't up to you to grit your teeth and try harder. Instead, he's given you the full power of the Holy Spirit to enable you to become the person he has created you to be. You can't do it alone. That is not his intention. His intention is that you become more and more dependent upon him. When you depend on his Holy Spirit, you will experience his supernatural power and freedom. See John 14:26; 16:13.

6. You have a new family of brothers and sisters in Christ who will help you grow in him. Just as our children go through different physical growth stages, you will go through different stages in your spiritual growth. You will need friends to whom you can go with your spiritual questions. No question, doubt, or feeling is silly or insignificant. You will be helped by having others who have "been there" to guide the way. I encourage you to seek out a church whose teachings are based on the authority of Scripture and to find a small group in which to be involved for encouragement. See 1 John 1:1–4 and 1 Thessalonians 5:11.

No longer do you have to *think* or *hope* or *wonder* if you are a believer. Now you are a *"know so"* believer. You *know so* because God promised he would come into your heart if you asked him to. And God keeps his promises.

Another thing you can *know* is that you can approach him *with confidence*! The Bible says, "In him [Jesus] and through faith in him we may approach God with freedom and confidence" (Eph. 3:12).

And so, dear friend, you and I can approach God with every single concern that we have about our teenager. Nothing is too silly. Nothing will shock him. Nothing is too difficult for him to handle. He longs for us to come to him and to share our heart with him just as you and I long for our teen to come and confide in us. He loves us even more than we love our child, so just imagine how much it thrills him when we come to him.

I pray that as you use this book to pray for your teen, your heart will be touched in a deep way with a fresh glimpse of how much your heavenly Father loves you.

Prayer for My Teen to Come to Faith

Dear friend, the following is a suggested prayer for you to use in praying for your child to come to faith. It stands alone, so if you choose, you can use it on a daily basis in addition to the "prayer of the day." However you choose to use this prayer, remember that Christ too is praying for your child! Romans 8:34 says, "Christ Jesus . . . is at the right hand of God and is also interceding for us"—*and therefore for your child*!

The greatest desire of a parent's heart is that our child would come to know Jesus Christ as personal Savior. It makes no difference if our teen is the epitome of a good kid in every way or a rebellious child who pushes every limit. She is still selfish (sinful) by nature. Only by accepting Christ's sacrifice on the cross for her sins can she begin to experience the abundant life he has for her and the power of the Holy Spirit with which to live it. Only then can she be assured that one day she will be in heaven with him—not because she is good or bad but because she is forgiven.

Father, my teen is far from you. She seems to have no interest in spiritual things. Oh, she's heard the truth about you, but she has chosen to ignore it. She's in control of her life (or at least she thinks she is!), and she'd rather fill her life with pleasures and plans of her own choosing than with any thoughts of you. She simply does not see a need in her own life for you.

This is hard, O Lord, because in many ways I feel like a failure. Father, I don't know what she's really thinking beneath the surface. I don't understand what has brought her to this place. What have I done or left undone?

You know how much I have agonized over my child. I know that the most important thing in her life needs to be you. But I cannot make her come to faith.

Father, as painful as this is for me, it is also good for me. I am reminded that I am weak.* Her faith or lack of faith is not dependent upon me, not dictated by what I have done or not done. Your power is far greater than any of my mistakes.*

Father, I now relinquish to you what's so precious to me, my child's faith. You long for her to know you even more than I do.* Your desire is greater than mine, and you alone have the power.* Thank you that this is not my burden to carry. You long to carry it for me.*

You are the one who loves her perfectly, who knows her intimately.* You alone can draw her to yourself.* You are the one who has promised to seek her, your little lost sheep.*

Father, today I ask that you would pursue her. Woo her to yourself as the bridegroom woos the bride.* Make her heart restless for you. Reveal to her a need for you. Bring her to the realization that only you can fill the gaps in her life. Put people in her path who know you. Cause them to reach out to her. Place reminders of yourself in her life today in surprising ways.

For this is what the Sovereign LORD says: I myself will search for my sheep and look after them. As a shepherd looks after his scattered flock when he is with them, so will I look after my sheep. I will rescue them from all the places where they were scattered on a day of clouds and darkness.

EZEKIEL 34:11–12

For nothing is impossible with God.

LUKE 1:37

Scripture references (in order of starred references in prayer): 2 Corinthians 12:9; Luke 1:37; 2 Peter 3:9 and Ephesians 1:19–20; Psalm 68:19; Psalm 139; John 12:32 and 6:45; Ezekiel 34:11–12; Revelation 22:17

APPENDIX 3

Creating a Driving Contract with Your Teen

The time when a teen gets his license is a scary time for the parent. Even though he may think he's competent, we know that he's inexperienced and therefore his reactions may not be quick. Developing driving instincts takes time.

The following is a suggested contract for a new driver. Such a contract has several benefits: Parents have to agree on their expectations; both the parents and the child will know clearly what is expected since it is written out and signed; the policy is agreed on in advance, which will lessen confrontations; and time is allowed for sharpening driving skills. This contract is designed to allow for a period in which your teen will have time to get some driving experience under his belt. Adjust this to fit your particular needs.

New Driver Contract

_____ (your teen's name) promises to Mom and Dad the following:

I will obey all speed limits.

I will not eat any food or consume any drinks while driving.

I will not play music loudly.

I will keep two hands on the wheel.

I will not have any passengers in the car until (date—I suggest a minimum of a month) except my siblings or parents. After this date, all arrangements to carry passengers need to be approved in advance by Mom and Dad.

If I receive a ticket, I will pay for it out of my own money.

I will only drive the car with permission from Mom or Dad. I will tell them where I am going and when I will be home. If I want to change my plans, I will call to get permission before I go anywhere.

I will not use the telephone while driving. If the phone rings, I will pull over to answer it. If I need to make a call, I will pull over.

Everyone in the car will wear seat belts or the car doesn't move.

The car can never hold more passengers than seat belts.

I may not drive on the following highways without permission: _____.

This contract can be changed to add or remove terms at any time if Mom and Dad and teen agree.

We, your parents, are proud of your progress and the sense of responsibility you have been showing.

Date: _____

Mom's signature   _____

Dad's signature   _____

Teen's signature   _____

For further help on this and other "hot topics," see chapter 6 of *And Then I Had Teenagers: Encouragement for Parents of Teens and Preteens.*

Helpful Resources

Books by Susan Alexander Yates and Family

And Then I Had Teenagers: Encouragement for Parents of Teens and Preteens

By Susan Alexander Yates (Grand Rapids: Baker, 2001)

This is the book from which the book you are holding evolved. It is designed to be your basic guide on parenting teens and preteens. In it I discuss the common challenges we face as we raise teens. Chapters include: Understanding This New Season *(What's normal, what's not?)*, Creating an Atmosphere of Encouragement (*Walking on eggshells?*), Building

Good Communication (*You just don't understand!*), Setting Limits and Letting Go (*Why can't you just trust me?*), Handling the "Hot Topics" (*Help! How should I handle sex, dating, media pressures, driving, drugs, etc.*). Taking Advantage of Peer Pressure (*But all my friends get to . . .*), Encouraging Your Teen's Faith (*I'm not sure I believe . . .*), Finding Hope When Things Don't Turn Out (*I never thought "it" would happen to me*), Helping Teens Choose the Right College or Job (*How am I supposed to know?*), and Training in Life Skills and Letting Go (*Leaving—is my child ready? Am I?*).

Questions at the end of each chapter make this book easy to use in a small group setting.

Audience: anyone with kids ages 10–20

Character Matters! Raising Kids with Values That Last

By John and Susan Yates (Grand Rapids: Baker, 2002)

In this book we highlight eight character traits that we want our kids to develop: integrity, a teachable spirit, self-discipline, compassion, a servant's heart, courage, faith, and joy. Character is developed in the everyday issues of life. We identify goals that will encourage these traits and suggest practical ways of achieving these goals. In the process parents will discover that we too need to grow in these same traits.

This book is easy to use in an adult Sunday school class or in a neighborhood small group. It has a complete leader's guide in the appendix as well as questions at the end of each chapter. It's excellent to use in an outreach ministry. We encourage you to include single parents in your small group.

Audience: anyone with kids ages 5–18

The Incredible Four-Year Adventure: Finding Real Faith, Fun, and Friendship at College

By John Yates and Chris Yates (Grand Rapids: Baker, 2000)

Written by two recent college graduates (my sons), this book is helpful to those high school students getting ready to go off to college. It takes an honest look at the common challenges students will face in that first year away, whether at a secular school or a Christian school. Thoughtful questions at the end of each chapter make it an excellent book to use in a group of high school seniors or college freshmen.

Audience: any high school junior or senior or college freshman; also gives valuable insight for the parent of a child heading to college

Other Helpful Resources

FOR PARENTS

Different Children, Different Needs

By Charles Boyd (Sisters, OR: Multnomah, 1994)

This book will teach you how to tailor your own unique parenting style to meet the different personalities of your children. It comes with a helpful study guide for use in a small group or as a couple.

Audience: parents with kids of any age

Parenting Today's Adolescent

By Dennis and Barbara Rainey (Nashville: Nelson, 1998)

This comprehensive book will guide parents through the minefields of media and modesty, among other subjects.

Scripturally based, hands-on, and encouraging advice will help parents negotiate these tumultuous years.

Audience: parents of preteens and teens

Guiding Your Teenagers (HomeBuilders Parenting Series)

By Dennis and Barbara Rainey (Little Rock: Family-Life, 2003)

This couples' Bible study will lead you through questions designed to illuminate biblical guidelines on parenting and how to apply them to your unique family situation. Weekly sessions and homework projects will bring you closer as a couple and define your parenting strategies. This study also includes advice on parent-teen interactions to help you plan dates with your teen to discuss such difficult subjects as sex, dating, peer pressure, and the media's influence.

Audience: parents of teens and preteens

How to Speak Alien

By Michael Ross (Kansas City, MO: Beacon Hill Press, 2001)

Discusses how to build strong relationships with your teenager.

Audience: parents of teens and preteens

Suddenly They're 13!

By David and Claudia Arp (Grand Rapids: Zondervan, 1999)

This book helps parents and adolescents make a positive transition into the teenage years.

Audience: parents of preteens

Adolescence Isn't Terminal

By Kevin Leman (Wheaton: Tyndale, 2002)

This book deals with some of the turbulent issues, including hate groups and suicide, which many face as they parent teens.

Audience: parents of teens, especially those struggling with difficult issues

Parents' Guide to the Spiritual Mentoring of Teens

By Joe White, Jim Weidmann (Wheaton: Tyndale, 2001)

This book is a valuable manual on how to disciple your teens.

Audience: parents of teens; youth workers

Parenting the Wild Child

By Miles McPherson (Minneapolis: Bethany, 2000)

Encouragement for parents dealing with rebellious teens.
Audience: parents of teens

Surviving the Prodigal Years

By Marcia Mitchell (Seattle: YWAM Publishing, 1999)

Encouragement for parents who are emotionally hurting over a child's waywardness.

Audience: parents in pain

She Calls Me Daddy

By Robert Wolgemuth (Colorado Springs: Focus on the Family Publications, 1996)

Encouragement for dads in building their relationship with their daughters.

Audience: fathers with daughters

Bringing Up Boys

By Dr. James Dobson (Wheaton: Tyndale, 2001)

Encouragement for parents with boys.
Audience: parents of sons

FOR TEENS

Starving

By Christie Pettit (Grand Rapids: Revell, 2003)

More than five million adolescent girls and women struggle with eating disorders, and more than 80 percent of American women are unhappy with their bodies. This book, written by a recent college graduate, is great to give your teen daughters. (Read it yourself too!) As a varsity tennis player at the University of Virginia, Christie struggled with anorexia. Her honest, compelling story offers encouragement and hope.
Audience: every young woman and her mom

The Fabric of Faithfulness

By Steve Garber (Downers Grove, IL: InterVarsity Press, 1996)

An excellent book for college students seeking to be faithful in their everyday lives.
Audience: high school seniors and college students

FOR PARENTS AND TEENS TOGETHER

So You're About to Be a Teenager

By Dennis and Barbara Rainey with their children Samuel and Rebecca Rainey (Nashville: Nelson, 2002)

This book, written by parents and teens, gives voice to the concerns that both preteens and teens need answers to but offers answers in a nonintimidating format. Discussion includes puberty, dating, sex, and purity.

Audience: parents and teens together

Passport to Purity

By Dennis and Barbara Rainey (Little Rock: Family-Life, 2001)

This set of audiotapes and workbooks includes everything you need for a weekend getaway to prepare your child for puberty and purity.

Audience: parents of preteens for use with their children

Teknon and the Champion Warriors and accompanying guidebooks

By Brent Sapp (Little Rock: FamilyLife, 2000)

Sessions based around engaging teen fiction help your son learn what it means to be a real man. Includes activities.

Audience: preteen boys and their dads

Susan Alexander Yates is a regular guest on *FamilyLife Today* and other national radio programs. Besides raising five children, she and her husband, John, speak about marriage and parenting throughout the country. Susan also is a regular contributor to *Today's Christian Woman*. John and Susan live in Falls Church, Virginia.